Deadly Denial: Xenophobia Governance and the Global Compact for Migration in South Africa

Jonathan Crush

SAMP MIGRATION POLICY SERIES NO. 82

Series Editor: Prof. Jonathan Crush

Southern African Migration Programme (SAMP)
2020

AUTHOR

Jonathan Crush is Professor at the Balsillie School of International Affairs, Waterloo, Canada, and Extraordinary Professor at the University of the Western Cape, Cape Town, South Africa.

© Southern African Migration Programme (SAMP) 2020

Published by the Southern African Migration Programme, International Migration Research Centre, Balsillie School of International Affairs, Waterloo, Ontario, Canada samponline.org

First published 2020

ISBN 978-1-920596-46-0

Cover photo by Kim Ludbrook for EPA

Production by Bronwen Dachs Muller, Cape Town

CONTENTS

	PAGE
Executive Summary	1
Introduction	3
Profiling Xenophobia	6
Governance by Displacement	13
Conclusion	18
References	21
Migration Policy Series	29

LIST OF TABLES

Table 1:	Comparative Citizen Attitudes Towards Immigration	6
Table 2:	Attitudes Towards Refugee Protection	8
Table 3:	Likelihood of Taking Action Against Migrants	8
Table 4:	South African Explanations for the Xenophobic Attacks on Migrants in 2008	8
Table 5:	Frequency of Collective Xenophobic Attacks	13

LIST OF FIGURES

Figure 1:	Xenophobia Intensity by Racial Group	11
Figure 2:	Xenophobia Intensity by Personal Income	11
Figure 3:	Xenophobia Intensity by Amount of Contact with Migrants	12

EXECUTIVE SUMMARY

The UN Global Compact for Safe, Orderly and Regular Migration commits signatories "to eliminate all forms of discrimination, condemn and counter expressions, acts and manifestations of racism, racial discrimination, violence, xenophobia and related intolerance against all migrants in conformity with international human rights law." To further this objective, states commit to establishing mechanisms to prevent, detect and respond to racial, ethnic and religious profiling of migrants by public authorities, as well as systematic instances of intolerance, xenophobia, racism and all other multiple and intersecting forms of discrimination; to promoting awareness-raising campaigns to inform public perceptions about the evidence-based positive contributions of migration, and to ending racism, xenophobia and stigmatization against all migrants. This commitment puts the onus on signatory governments, including South Africa, to deal with the threat that increasingly accompanies global mobility and migration, that is, rising xenophobia in countries of migrant destination.

The character, drivers, impacts and policy responses to xenophobia have been topics of recurrent research interest in recent decades, most of it focused on negative attitudes towards and the discriminatory treatment of migrants in Europe and North America. Much less attention has been paid to xenophobia in the migrant-receiving countries and regions of the Global South. This mirrors a broader research and international policy lack of interest in South-South migration and its role in the development of countries of origin and destination. At the same time, evidence of intensifying xenophobic sentiment in the South is accumulating in disparate settings including in India, Singapore, the Gulf, Latin America and the Caribbean, and several West African and Southern African countries.

In the Global South, governance responses to anti-immigrant sentiment and action take three main forms: indifference, intensification and (occasionally) mitigation. In South Africa, policy on international migration suggests a fourth possibility: xenophobia denialism, displacement of responsibility onto shadowy criminals and blaming migrants for their own victimization. Here government focuses more on the perceived negative impacts of migration than any potential development benefits. As a result, negativity pervades policy discourse about migrants and their impact on the country. Migrants themselves have encountered an extremely hostile environment in which their constitutional and legal rights are abrogated, their ability to access basic services and resources is constrained, and their very presence in the country is excoriated by the state and the citizenry. Xenophobic attitudes are deeply entrenched in South Africa and xenophobic attacks have become common. This report first examines the research evidence from the last 20 years to support this conclusion and to show what government attempts to explain away through denial and displacement.

Xenophobic attacks are certainly criminal but they are not generally perpetrated by organized crime or habitual criminals. Government has also shown a marked disinclination to identify, pursue and prosecute the perpetrators of these criminal acts. An obvious objection to this characterization of South Africa's governance response is the acceptance by Cabinet in 2019 of a long-awaited National Action Plan to Combat, Racial Discrimination, Xenophobia and Related Intolerance. This plan, which fulfilled a long-overdue commitment to develop and implement the Declaration and Programme of Action adopted by the 2001 UN World Conference Against Racial Discrimination, Xenophobia and Related Intolerance in Durban, was riven with internal debate about whether xenophobia should even be included. The Plan is extremely light on detail, treating xenophobia in a perfunctory manner, providing no information about the nature and extent of the phenomenon, and proposing few steps to deal with it. Any proposed remedies are largely reactive rather than proactive. With official policies of xenophobia denial and displacement in place, there seems little chance that South Africa will address one of the core commitments of the Global Compact on Migration; that is, "to, condemn and counter expressions, acts and manifestations of…xenophobia and related intolerance." Indeed, if (as official policy contends) xenophobia does not exist, then, by definition, there is nothing to condemn and counter. In this environment, the consequences for migrants themselves will continue to be extremely deleterious and deadly.

INTRODUCTION

The UN Global Compact for Safe, Orderly and Regular Migration (UN, 2018) has recently been labelled a depoliticized document marked by major internal contradictions (Pécoud, 2020). There is at least one respect, however, in which it is neither contradictory nor depoliticized; that is, in the agreement of signature states to eliminate all forms of discrimination against migrants and their families. Objective 17.33 of the Global Compact makes a commitment "to eliminate all forms of discrimination, condemn and counter expressions, acts and manifestations of racism, racial discrimination, violence, xenophobia and related intolerance against all migrants in conformity with international human rights law" (UN, 2018). To further this objective, states commit to establish mechanisms "to prevent, detect and respond to racial, ethnic and religious profiling of migrants by public authorities, as well as systematic instances of intolerance, xenophobia, racism and all other multiple and intersecting forms of discrimination" and promote awareness-raising campaigns to inform public perceptions about the evidence-based positive contributions of migration, and "to end racism, xenophobia and stigmatization against all migrants." This may be idealistic and unachievable, but is certainly not contradictory or depoliticized, putting the onus on states to deal with evidence of a growing challenge accompanying increased global mobility and migration: the growth of xenophobia in countries of migrant destination.

The character, drivers, impacts and policy responses to xenophobia have been topics of recurrent interest in recent decades, generating a sizable literature, most of it focused on negative attitudes towards and the discriminatory treatment of migrants in Europe and North America (d'Appollonia, 2017; Gorinas and Pytliková, 2018; Peterie and Neal, 2020; Rensmann and Miller, 2017). Much less attention has been paid to xenophobia in the migrant-receiving countries and regions of the Global South (Crush and Ramachandran, 2010). This mirrors a broader research and international policy disinterest in South-South migration and its role in the development of countries of origin and destination (Fiddian-Qasmiyeh, 2020). At the same time, evidence of intensifying xenophobic sentiment in the Global South is beginning to accumulate in disparate settings including in India (Adibe 2017; Ramachandran, 2019), Singapore (Gomes, 2014; Yang, 2017), the Gulf (Ullah et al., 2020), Latin America and the Caribbean (Gill and Danns, 2018; Meseguer and Kemmerling, 2018; Jones, 2020), and several West African and Southern African countries (Akinola, 2018; Miran-Guyon, 2016; Campbell and Crush, 2015; Crush and Pendleton, 2007; Whitaker, 2015). One extremely common xenophobic trope associates migrants with threats to the health of citizens by bringing disease and using up scarce health resources. There is evidence, for example, of an upsurge in COVID-19-related xenophobic reaction across the South (Ahuja et al., 2020; Castillo and Amoah, 2020; Chan and Strabucchi, 2020; Reny and Barreto, 2020). The significance of the new literature prompted by the pandemic is that it draws close attention to the politics of xenophobia and, in particular, the ways in which the national and local state is implicated in its development, reinforcement and reproduction.

State responses to evidence of xenophobia in the general population range across a broad terrain but include mitigation (rare), indifference (more common) and intensification (extremely common). Populist political parties invariably embed anti-immigrant rhetoric and policy proposals in their election platforms and, if and when they come to power, enact policies that are demonstrably xenophobic. The Hindu right Bharatiya Janata Party (BJP) in India, for example, has long advocated a punitive approach to "infiltrators" from neighbouring states and has enacted a range of new policies designed to exclude millions of Muslim migrants (both internal and international) (Ramachandran, 2019). In post-colonial Africa, as Fourchard and Segatti (2015: 6) point out, "the attention paid to exclusionary discourses and practices that haunt the politics of belonging throughout the continent is not always balanced by an interest in countervailing discourses and practices (reconciliation, diffusing ethnic oppositions, everyday conviviality etc.)." The main reason for the low interest in countervailing discourses is that there are few, if any, good examples to study. The nation-building projects of most post-colonial states focus more on the perceived threats to national sovereignty and citizen livelihoods posed by migrants, refugees and immigrants. Opportunities to take up permanent residence and citizenship in other countries are also extremely constrained.

Recurrent violence targeting foreign nationals in South Africa has been debated at length without much consensus about its fundamental causes (Gordon, 2020a; Hassim et al., 2008; Landau, 2012; Matsinhe, 2016; Neocosmos, 2010; Nyamnjoh, 2006; Steinberg, 2012, 2018; Tevera, 2013; Misago, 2016). Less attention has been paid to the responses and associated ways of speaking about xenophobia by national, provincial and municipal governments and whether these responses mitigate or exacerbate xenophobia and/or license acts of violence (Crush et al., 2013; Hiropoulos, 2020; Misago, 2017; Musuva, 2015). In terms of the proposed governance typology, are state responses to xenophobia in South Africa characterized by indifference, intensification or mitigation or something else? The South African case suggests that there is a fourth alternative in the typology of governance responses to xenophobia: that is, governance by denial and displacement. This can take a variety of forms including denial that xenophobia exists and is a problem – which we have labelled elsewhere as 'xenophobia denialism' (Crush and Ramachandran, 2014) – and displacing blame for mounting evidence of xenophobic attitudes and actions onto migrants themselves (based on a series of negative stereotypes of migrants as criminals, job-stealers and resource consumers) or onto the criminal behaviour of anti-social and marginalized citizens.

This report focuses primarily on national government responses to xenophobia in South Africa and argues that denial and displacement best characterize the reactions of government to evidence of post-1994 xenophobic attitudes and instances of xenophobic behaviour. Policies and discourses of intensification have been more evident at sub-national provincial and local level, most notably in Limpopo, North West Province, KwaZulu-Natal and the city of Johannesburg (Masuku, 2016; Mothibi et al., 2015; Ngcamu and Mantzaris, 2019). Gauteng Premier David Makhura recently claimed that "we are cleaning up our [CBD]. We will not rest until we take our city back" as he joined police in raids that resulted in the arrests of hundreds of migrants (HRW, 2020: 43). Former Johannesburg Mayor Herman Mashaba has repeatedly castigated migrants for their supposed "takeover" of the city, blaming them for all manner of social and economic ills and exhibiting "violent impunity through raids and evictions, particularly in Johannesburg's inner city. He reinforced xenophobia and deepened inequality while creating a fabled narrative as a unifier with business acumen" (Johnson, 2020).

The first section of the report reviews the evidence for the existence and persistence of xenophobic attitudes and violence in the country. The next section provides an overview of the violence that appears to the victims and most independent commentators to be motivated by xenophobia. The report then turns to the South African government and its policy of denial and displacement as a response to xenophobia. It concludes with a discussion of the implications for implementing the Global Compact commitments to eliminating xenophobia in the country.

PROFILING XENOPHOBIA

In the absence of globally comparative surveys of public opinion, it is difficult to say if South Africa is exceptional or typical in its antagonistic response to immigration and immigrants. Wave 6 of the World Values Survey (2010-2014) provides a preliminary answer around the single common question in all its representative country surveys about attitudes to government allowing migrants into the country and under what conditions. Table 1 clearly shows that South Africans have the most negative attitudes towards immigration of all Global South countries surveyed. As many as 30% want borders completely closed (the same as India), while 78% support closed borders and strict limits on entry (compared to only 55% in India). Only Malaysia, Thailand and Indonesia have comparable or greater scores on both metrics combined. SAMP has conducted three national surveys of South African attitudes towards migrants, refugees and migration policies (in 1998, 2006 and 2010) in which the same question elicited very similar results for South Africa (Crush, 2001, 2008; Crush et al., 2013; Dambrun et al., 2006; Debrosee et al., 2016). The survey also collected representative data on a broad range of attitudes and their demographic, social, economic and cultural determinants.

TABLE 1: Comparative Citizen Attitudes Towards Immigration

Country	Prohibit entry (%)	Strict limits (%)	As long as jobs available (%)	Let anyone come (%)
South Africa	30	48	16	6
India	30	25	22	23
Egypt	26	43	25	5
Jordan	25	46	28	2
Malaysia	18	72	8	2
Mexico	17	25	45	12
Zambia	15	44	30	11
Thailand	14	65	16	5
Morocco	11	20	41	28
Brazil	11	33	47	9
Trinidad & Tobago	10	55	32	4
Chile	9	35	50	6

China	8	21	51	20
Indonesia	8	72	15	6
Guatemala	7	21	55	17
Ghana	6	36	39	18
Peru	6	21	50	23
Argentina	6	34	45	15
Ethiopia	5	27	28	40
Mali	4	16	46	34

Source: http://www.worldvaluessurvey.org/WVSDocumentationWV6.jsp

Previous reports in this SAMP series captured a wide range of negative attitudes and perceptions relating to migrants, migration and immigration policy in the 1990s and 2000s (Crush, 2001, 2008; Crush et al., 2013). The 2010 SAMP survey provided extensive insights into the attitudes of South Africans towards migrants and refugees, their willingness to take action against migrants in their neighbourhood, and their stereotyping of the adverse consequences of immigration (Crush et al., 2013). Table 2, for example, shows the strong opposition to the country taking in more refugees (57% opposed/11% supportive), using taxpayer money to support refugees (46% opposed/16% supportive), and granting permanent residence to long-term refugees (44% opposed/18% supportive). There was also strong support for repatriating refugees when they are no longer at risk (56% supportive/14% opposed) and mandatory HIV testing for all refugees (41% supportive/ 29% opposed). As Table 3 shows, around one-third of South Africans said they would take various actions against migrants in their neighbourhood, with 15% prepared to force migrants to leave the area and 11% to use violence to achieve his end. The survey also asked South Africans why they thought the 2008 nationwide violence against migrants had occurred. Around two-thirds of the residents of hotspots (areas that had experienced violence) blamed migrants for the mayhem by their engaging in crime, taking jobs from locals and being culturally different. More than half said they brought it on themselves by using health services for free and "stealing women" (a misogynistic reference to intermarriage between migrants and South Africans) (Table 4). As many as 62% agreed that "migrants do not belong in South Africa."

TABLE 2: Attitudes Towards Refugee Protection

	Support (%)	Oppose (%)
Grant asylum to those escaping war and persecution	38	23
Increase refugee intake in South Africa	11	57
Grant permanent residence to refugees in South Africa for > 5 years	18	44
Send refugees back when they are no longer at risk	56	13
Refugees must live in special camps near the border	31	32
Use government budget to look after refugees	14	46
Allow refugees to work in South Africa	25	35
Test refugees for HIV	41	29

TABLE 3: Likelihood of Taking Action Against Migrants

	% Likely	% Unlikely
Report them to police	36	39
Report them to employer	27	45
Report them to community association	27	45
Combine to force them to leave	15	73
Use violence against them	11	72

TABLE 4: South African Explanations for the Xenophobic Attacks on Migrants in 2008

Reasons for the attacks:	% agree	% disagree
They cause crime in South Africa	64	11
They take jobs from South Africans	62	16
They are culturally different	60	14
They cheat South Africans	56	14
They do not belong in South Africa	56	17
They use health services for free	55	15
They take government-subsidized houses from South Africans	52	17
The men 'steal' South African women	52	19
South African criminals are to blame	32	27
The police do not protect them	27	37

Other contemporaneous attitudinal surveys confirmed that anti-migrant and refugee sentiment was widespread (Gordon, 2015, 2016a, 2016b; Claassen, 2017; Gordon and Maharaj, 2015). The key question is whether the anti-migrant sentiment of the immediate post-apartheid period has persisted to the present. Evidence from annual South African Social Attitudes Survey (SASA) suggests that it has. Although SASA only asks a handful of questions about migration (and does not ask the same questions every year), the data suggests that there has not been any significant diminution in hostility since 2010 (Dube, 2018, 2019; Gordon 2017a, 2017b, 2020a, 2020b; Reudin, 2019). As Gordon (2018) notes, SASA data indicates considerable "durability of public attitudes towards international immigrants" over the last decade. Dube (2019) tracks South African attitudes to openness to immigration between 2008 and 2016 and shows that after an initial decline between 2008 and 2010, attitudes stabilized for the rest of the period. Data from the 2014 SASA shows that more than 75% of South Africans associated immigrants with increased crime rates, taking jobs from locals and spreading disease (Gordon 2018). Using data from the 2015-2017 surveys, Gordon (2019) found that a significant number were prepared to resort to violence against migrants. In 2015, the equivalent of "almost 5 million adult South Africans reported that while they had not previously participated in violent action against international migrants, they were prepared to consider doing so in the future" (Gordon 2010a:108). SASA 2018 provides insights into the rationale for anti-migrant violence which has continued virtually unabated over the last decade. The actions of migrants were viewed as the main cause of the violence while the expulsion of migrants was viewed as the most appropriate response to solve the issue (Gordon, 2019: 5). A different data source – the 2019 SA Reconciliation Barometer – found that a significant minority of South Africans were likely or very likely to prevent people from other African countries accessing commercial spaces (39%), the workplace or schools (38%), social gatherings (37%), or public recreation (34%). Almost 40% reported that they were likely to prevent people from other African countries from moving into their neighbourhood, or from operating a business in their area (38%). Just over one-third reported that they were likely to prevent people from other African countries from accessing government services (34%), and from accessing jobs (36%) (Potgieter, 2020: 69-70).

Rather than focusing on attitudes towards a particular aspect of migration, some researchers have developed composite indices that combine different questions to provide overall measures of anti-migration attitudes These include the Perceived Foreign Threat

Index and Perceived Foreign Benefit Index (Gordon, 2017a), the Immigration Consequence Index (Gordon, 2018), and the Additive Scale of Anti-Immigrant Attitudes (Ruedin, 2019). While these measures have real value in the search for statistically significant relationships with possible causal factors, they rely on a small set of questions, and rightly do not claim to be measures of xenophobia writ large. The only attempt to derive a more holistic xeno-phobia metric to date is SAMP's Xenophobia Index (SXI) which is based on a dedicated migration survey instrument with numerous questions capturing different aspects of atti-tudes towards migration to and migrants within South Africa (de la Sablonnière et al., 2007; Auger et al., 2011).

To calculate the SXI principal components analysis was used to identify items from the questionnaire that evaluated the same concept or construct. Nine questions relating to the "favourability rating" of different categories of migrant rated on a scale from 0 (very favour-able) to 10 (very unfavourable) fit this criterion. Six composite scales were then calculated using the 2006 and 2010 survey data using slightly different methods (e.g. weighting and unweighting the data). The stability of all six scales was assessed by performing correlations between them and other variables related to xenophobic attitudes on particular issues. All six scales could be used but the SXI is based on the most stable "xeno2" scale which gener-ates a score for each individual on a scale between 0 and 10 for each respondent. SXI means are then calculated and cross-tabulated by racial group, age group, education, income level, employment status, and so on. Figures 1 to 3 cross-tabulate the SXI with three of the many possible independent variables (race, income and amount of contact with migrants). Apart from the high overall levels of xenophobia, there are notable variations in the intensity of xenophobic sentiment by racial group (with Black South Africans being least xenophobic and Indian/Asian South Africans most xenophobic), by household income (with levels of xenophobia increasing with household income), and by amount of contact with migrants (with levels of xenophobia decreasing with increased amounts of contact). The SXI did not vary significantly with age, sex, education, residence or employment status of citizens. A follow-up study using the SXI is highly desirable and would show whether there has been a reduction, increase or stabilization of overall levels of xenophobia.

FIGURE 1: Xenophobia Intensity by Racial Group

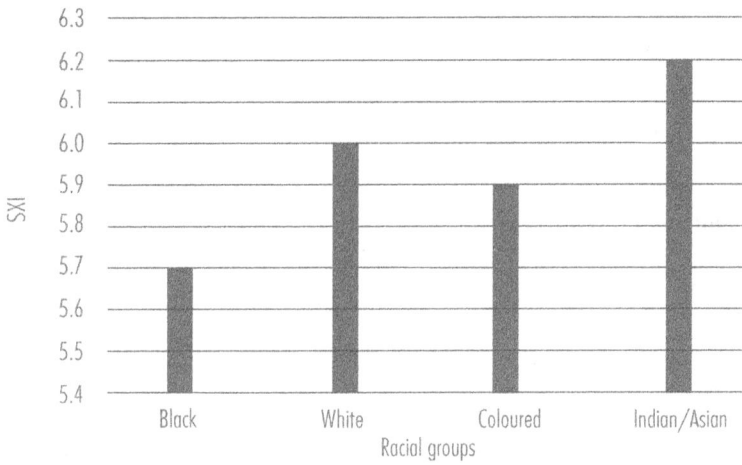

FIGURE 2: Xenophobia Intensity by Personal Income

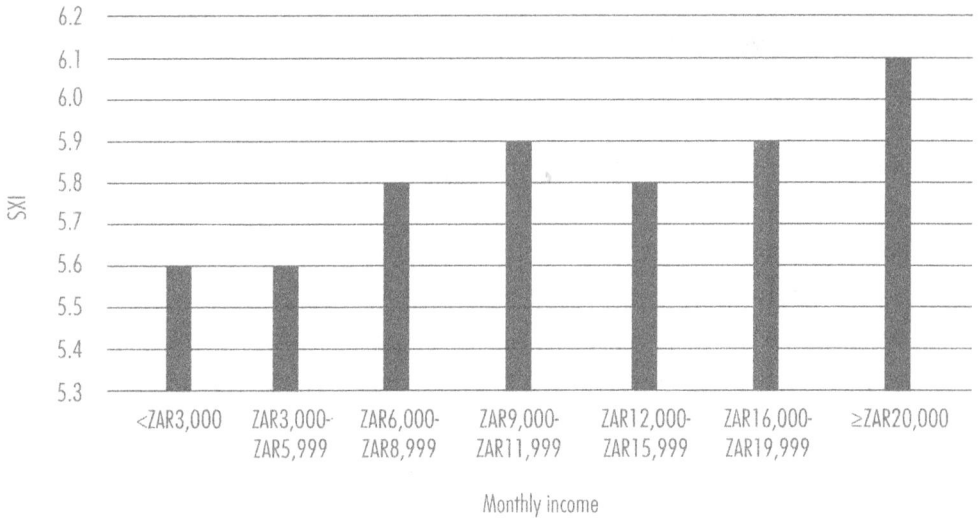

FIGURE 3: Xenophobia Intensity by Amount of Contact with Migrants

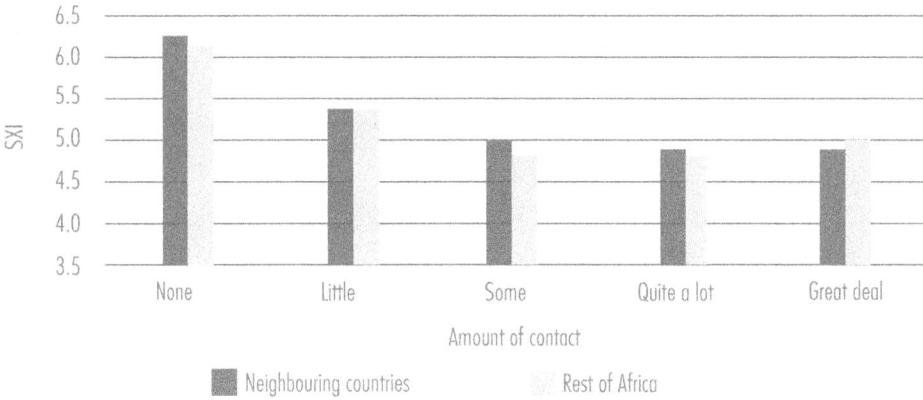

Xenophobic attitudes have translated readily into routinized xenophobic behaviour involving exclusionary language, verbal denigration, denial of access to services such as health and education, and insistent demands from citizens that government rid their communities and the country of "foreigners." Xenophobic attitudes have also been closely linked to xenophobic actions including collective violence targeting migrants and refugees. South Africa experienced intense nationwide rounds of violence in 2008, 2015 and again in 2019 (Bekker, 2015; Burke, 2019; Desai, 2015; Hayem, 2013). These moments of ethnic cleansing represent "a heightened form of xenophobia in which hostility and opposition to those perceived as outsiders and foreigners is strongly embedded and expressed through aggressive acts directed at migrants and refugees (and) recurrent episodes of violence" (Crush and Ramachandran, 2015).

Collective violence also manifests on an almost daily basis in particular localities with the looting and destruction of migrant-owned businesses in the informal sector and injury and murder of business owners and their employees (Crush et al., 2015; Ramachandran et al., 2017). Episodes of collective violence targeting small businesses include combinations of written or verbal threats and insults, public intimidation through protests or marches, forced shop closures, physical assaults and murder of migrant store owners or their employees, looting of store contents, arson or other damage to the shop structure, damage or destruction of the business property including homes and vehicles, temporary or permanent forced displacement and extortion for protection by local leaders, police and residents. Crush and Ramachandran (2015) documented 220 episodes of collective violence against migrant and refugee businesses in various locations around the country between 2005 and 2014 (excluding the violence of 2008). The frequency of collective violence has increased over time (Table 5). In December 2018, the Xenowatch monitoring group reported 529 xenophobic violence incidents in post-apartheid South Africa resulting in 309 deaths, 901 physical assaults, 2,193 shops looted and over 100,000 people displaced (Mlilo and Misago, 2019).

TABLE 5: Frequency of Collective Xenophobic Attacks

Year	No. of incidents	% of total
Pre-2005	9	4
2005	4	2
2006	9	4
2007	9	4
2008	19	8
2009	17	7
2010	46	20
2011	22	10
2012	25	11
2013	36	16
2014 (to end-August)	32	14
Total	228	100
Source: Crush and Ramachandran (2015a)		

GOVERNANCE BY DISPLACEMENT

The dominant response of the South African national government to the undeniable existence of xenophobia is governance by denial and displacement. First, with regard to xenophobia denialism, the Mandela and Mbeki governments did little to acknowledge or address growing xenophobia in the late 1990s and early 2000s (Crush, 2001). However, in 2006, the report on South Africa by the African Union's African Peer Review Mechanism (APRM) said that xenophobia was a serious issue for South Africa and urged the government to tackle it through concerted action (AU, 2006: 24). This occurred at the same historical moment that Mbeki was espousing pan-Africanism and the idea of an

African renaissance, on the one hand, and promoting the HIV and AIDS denialism that cost hundreds of thousands of South African lives, on the other (Fassin and Schneider, 2003; Mbongmba, 2004). As Dodson and Crush (2016: 288) point out, "xenophobia could not readily be accommodated within Mbeki's discourse of an African Renaissance and was therefore simply denied, either by him or on behalf of his 'people.'" Xenophobia denialism was also entirely consistent with the tendency to ignore scientific evidence and avoid taking responsibility for catastrophic social outcomes (Nattrass, 2003).

Against the backdrop of mounting African Union and international scrutiny and condemnation, Mbeki denied any connection between attacks on migrants and xenophobia. Xenophobia denialism became official government policy and was initially deployed to explain away nationwide violence against migrants and refugees in 2008. In a public address meant to commemorate the more than 60 people who had died, Mbeki announced that he had never met a xenophobic South African. Further, he stated, anyone who called South Africans xenophobic was themself guilty of xenophobia: "None in our society has any right to encourage or incite xenophobia by trying to explain naked criminal activity by cloaking it in the garb of xenophobia" (Mbeki, 2008). The idea that these actions were the result of "naked criminality", not xenophobia, took root and became a central plank in state orthodoxy that continues to the present (Gerber, 2019). His successors abandoned HIV and AIDS denialism, but reinforced xenophobia denialism. From 2008 onwards, politicians from the ruling party carefully avoided the term xenophobia when referring to violence against migrants and blamed it instead on criminality. However, as some have pointed out, the rate of arrest and prosecution of these "criminals" over the years has been abysmal (HRW, 2019).

In 2010, the Minister of Police characterized attacks against migrants as "crimes of opportunity" where criminal or anti-social elements "take advantage of the situation to engage in such misdeeds" (Sapa, 2010). Commenting after a Zimbabwean migrant was stoned to death in 2011, police spokesperson Zweli Mnisi echoed this view: "Once you start talking about xenophobia and Afrophobia, you are talking about semantics. It is crime disguised under xenophobia" (Isaacson, 2011). On another occasion, Mnisi is quoted as saying that "holistically speaking, South Africans are not xenophobic and many cases are merely crime" (Bauer, 2013). In mid-2013, following an upsurge of violent assaults on Somali refugees, then Minister of International Relations and Cooperation, Maite Nkoana-Mashabane, announced that "the looting, displacement and killing of foreign nationals in South Africa should not be viewed as xenophobic attacks, but opportunistic criminal acts that have the potential to undermine the unity and cohesiveness of our communities" (Patel, 2013). The South African Cabinet also issued a public statement on the violence, noting that "Cabinet is cautious not to label this violence as xenophobia because preliminary evidence indicates that these acts may be driven primarily by criminality" (RSA, 2013).

At an African Union meeting in Johannesburg in June 2015, then President Jacob Zuma reiterated the government's position by arguing that "South Africans are not xenophobic. We do not believe that the actions of a few out of more than 50 million citizens justify the label of xenophobia" (Du Plessis, 2015). Zuma also publicly declared that "millions of peace loving South Africans are in pain also because they are being accused of xenophobia, which is not true. South Africans are definitely not xenophobic (Zuma, 2015). In a Parliamentary debate following an upsurge of xenophobic violence in late 2019, Defence Minister Nosiviwe Mapisa-Nqakula restated the official line that the attacks were "mostly acts of criminality irrespective of the nationality of those involved. Crime is crime. It is not South African to hate thy neighbour." In the same debate Police Minister Bheki Cele stated that "for us it's nothing to do with xenophobia, it is criminality" (Gerber, 2019).

The second component of governance by denial and displacement is scapegoating or assigning blame for the violence to migrants themselves. In 2015, for example, Mapisa-Nqakula expanded the definition of criminality to include migrant "criminals": "While government is going to be taking resolute actions against South Africans who attack foreign nationals, we are equally determined to take action against all foreign nationals who commit crime in our country" (Merten, 2015). High-ranking ruling party official Gwede Mantashe openly blamed the rising numbers of migrants for the violence and said the solution was the "tightening [of] immigration laws" and "if need be, establish refugee camps" to geographically segregate migrants from citizens (Finnan, 2015). However, scapegoating has been most evident in government responses to the country's recurrent episodes of violence, looting and destruction of the premises of migrants and refugees operating small informal businesses (called spazas) in the informal sector. First, an Inter-Ministerial Committee (IMC) on Migration housed in the Presidency was constituted in 2015. Fifteen government ministers sat on the IMC, an indication of how seriously government viewed the crisis. The official brief of the IMC was "to promote orderly and efficient migration and peaceful co-existence between citizens and non-South Africans, as well as to consider social, economic and security aspects of migration" (PJC, 2015: 19). Second, a parliamentary committee was constituted with the mandate to investigate the causes of the violence (the Ad Hoc Parliamentary Committee Probing Violence Against Foreign Nationals) (PJC, 2015).

The Chair of the IMC at the time, Minister Jeff Radebe, briefed the parliamentary ad hoc committee on the findings, stating that the primary cause of the violence against foreign nationals was "increased competition arising from the socio-economic circumstances in South Africa" and the "business models used by migrants to discourage competition such as forming monopolies, evading taxes, avoiding customs and selling illegal and expired goods" (PMG, 2015). Competition had been heightened by "a decade of poor implementation of immigration and border controls." Further, foreign nationals were placing a strain on government services such as health, housing, education and social grants and "dominating trade in certain sectors such as consumable goods in informal settlements which has had a negative impact on unemployed and low skilled South Africans." He also blamed the victims for the attacks: "They roam, they go to townships to occupy the economic space. We never invaded economic space in exile" (News24, 2015). At a press conference he further observed that "as the Inter-Ministerial Committee, we've concluded that South Africans are not xenophobic" (Davis, 2015).

The parliamentary ad hoc committee's investigation went even further, repeatedly asserting that xenophobia as a phenomenon did not exist in South Africa (News24, 2015; Nicolson, 2015; PJC, 2015). The committee claimed that South Africans do not hate migrants and refugees and in the parliamentary deliberations leading up to the adoption of the report, it was recommended that the term "xenophobia" be omitted because no convincing evidence had apparently been found that the phenomenon even existed (PMG, 2015). The final report notes that "Parliament had not yet come to the conclusion that the incidents of violence against foreign nationals were due to xenophobia as per the dictionary definition of extreme, irrational hatred of foreign nationals" (PJC, 2015). The parliamentary committee concluded that "the main causes of the violent attacks were criminal actions that started with stealing of goods from foreign owned spaza shops by South African criminals who are often drug addicts. The spaza shop owners would react by shooting at those who steal from their spaza shops using unregistered firearms rather than reporting to the police. When this happens and someone is killed, local communities retaliate by looting spaza shops owned by foreign nationals rather than reporting to the police" (PJC, 2015: 35).

The idea that migrant spaza owners were responsible, by their very presence, for the attacks on their persons and premises resonated strongly with the views of many citizens and beyond.

Independent commissions of enquiry, such as the Special Reference Group on Migration and Community Integration in KwaZulu-Natal (SRG) headed by the former UN High Commissioner for Refugees, argued that the immediate cause of the outbreak was "deliberate efforts of select individuals, some of whom had interests in the informal trading sector, to drive away competition by foreign national-owned businesses…These deliberate efforts sparked the outbreak of widespread incidents of criminality, violence and looting of properties owned by foreign nationals." Furthermore, "many of the perceptions of foreign national traders, although largely unfounded, contributed to heightened tensions" (SRG, 2015: x). However, the SRG studiously avoided labelling the violence "xenophobic" or seeing xenophobia as a contributing or motivating factor. At most, it conceded that "the violent attacks against foreign nationals were, in some measure, fuelled by dominant and negative perceptions that exist amongst locals and foreign nationals about one another" (SRG, 2015). However, it is difficult to see how the attitudes of foreign nationals could be responsible for their own victimization. Also, none of the mob violence was perpetrated by migrants on South Africans. An anti-xenophobia protest march organized by NGOs and migrant groups to Durban's City Hall on 7 April 2015 was declared illegal and the police used water cannons, teargas and rubber bullets to disperse the crowd (Ngubane, 2015).

In April 2015, in the wake of the violence, the IMC implemented its controversial and militaristic "Operation Fiela." Operation Fiela was described on the government website as "a multidisciplinary interdepartmental operation aimed at eliminating criminality and general lawlessness from our communities. As the word 'Fiela' means to sweep clean, we are ridding communities of crime and criminals so that the people of South Africa can be and feel safe. The ultimate objective of the operation is to create a safe and secure environment for all in South Africa." The central objective of Operation Fiela was not, in fact, to protect migrants or arrest the perpetrators of violence. Instead it launched a nationwide campaign by the police and army to harass migrant-owned businesses, to locate undocumented migrants and to arrest and deport them. By the end of 2015, government boasted that Operation Fiela had searched 460,000 people, 151,000 vehicles and 38,000 premises. A total of 41,000 arrests had also been made. Between April and June 2015, 10,242 migrants were deported, of which Zimbabweans constituted more than one-quarter (SRG, 2015). The absence of due process in Operation Fiela prompted Lawyers for Human Rights to (unsuccessfully) challenge its constitutionality in the North Gauteng High Court in June 2015. An application for leave to appeal to the Constitutional Court was dismissed in December 2016 (Constitutional Court, 2016). Lawyers for Human Rights characterized Operation Fiela as "state-sponsored xenophobia" and "institutional xenophobia" that blurred stark differences between criminals and migrants, "while deepening the divide between citizens and foreigners by bolstering negative perceptions, instead of correcting them" (Jordaan, 2015; LHR, 2015).

CONCLUSION

The global migration and development agenda puts great emphasis on the positive development impacts of migration. As the former UN Special Representative for International Migration, Louise Arbour, noted, there exists a global "virtuous circle" in which "migration is overwhelmingly positive for migrants and their communities, both origin and destination (and) a potent motor of development" (Arbour, 2018). To achieve these outcomes, governments and citizenries need to openly recognize and acknowledge the existence of this virtuous circle, work assiduously to ensure its realization, and remove institutional and attitudinal obstacles that stand in the way. In post-apartheid South Africa, there has been little recognition of the positive relationship between migration and development, much less concrete efforts to mainstream development in migration policy and migration in development policy. The country's omnibus 2030 National Development Plan does make isolated references to the need for greater openness for skilled migrants and a "more progressive" immigration policy (NPC, 2012). On just one occasion it observes that well-managed migration can "contribute positively to South Africa's development" but this is followed almost immediately by a statement about the burden of migration (NPC, 2012: 105). And there is no systematic plan for how to make migration work for development other than by recruiting high-level skills. The 2017 White Paper on International Migration, still unimplemented, claims to be that plan and does give lip-service to the migration-development relationship (DHA, 2017). However, its managerial framework focuses more on how to better control, monitor and manage migration and refugee flows. Neither mentions xenophobia as an obstacle to the development of a well-managed migration system, much less making migration work for development.

A major under-explored barrier to realizing the full development benefits of migration is the negative attitudes, shading into passive and active xenophobia, among the citizenry of migrant destination states. In this context, the South African case has particular relevance. While the country occupies an unenviable position at one extreme of the spectrum of negative attitudes to migration, xenophobia is also a growing phenomenon in many countries of the North and South. In South Africa, as this report suggests, there is incontrovertible evidence that xenophobia is rife throughout the country and in the corridors of state. State responses to xenophobia vary considerably but can basically be distilled into four models of governance; indifference, mitigation, intensification and denial/displacement. South Africa has eschewed mitigation and, unlike in countries where populism is on the rise, national political parties have not yet sought to use anti-migrant hostility as a central policy platform, thus promoting and intensifying xenophobia. Instead, the South African response has been characterized by denial and displacement; first, in the face of ferocious collective violence against migrants, government denies that xenophobia exists or is responsible in any way for the mayhem. Blame is invariably displaced onto criminals and criminality. While the acts are certainly criminal, they are not generally perpetrated by organized crime or habitual criminals but by members of local communities of all ages. Since 2015, however, blame has increasingly been displaced onto migrants themselves, not least by government ministers on the influential IMC in the Presidency that launched a punitive campaign against migrants in the aftermath of collective xenophobic violence.

One obvious objection to this characterization of the governance response is the acceptance by Cabinet of a long-awaited National Action Plan to Combat, Racial Discrimination, Xenophobia and Related Intolerance (RSA, 2019). This plan, which took nearly twenty years of internal foot-dragging to complete, finally fulfilled a longstanding commitment made by South Africa to develop and implement the Declaration and Programme of Action adopted by the 2001 UN World Conference Against Racial Discrimination, Xenophobia and Related Intolerance in Durban. Earlier drafts of the Plan removed any reference to xenophobia entirely. The fact that it has finally seen the light of day, could be read as signalling that Government has finally accepted that xenophobia is a real phenomenon and needs to be combatted. However, government ministers have simultaneously continued to deny the existence of xenophobia and to displace blame onto criminals and migrants themselves. The plan itself treats xenophobia in a perfunctory manner, providing no information about the nature and extent of the phenomenon and proposing no proactive steps to deal with it.

The proposed remedies are largely reactive: condemning violence when it occurs, enacting hate crime laws, strengthening law enforcement and prosecuting offenders. One sentence is devoted to the need to monitor and report on attacks and another to "promote a spirit of integration through engaging communities where xenophobia is rampant." The primary concrete measure proposed is to implement the recommendations of the Parliamentary Joint Committee and the SRG Report (RSA, 2019: 61). It remains to be seen whether government will act on the SRG's more progressive and proactive remedies (SRG, 2015: 172-178) or the calls for greater controls on migration and disadvantaging migrant businesses proposed by the parliamentary committee (2015: 36-39).

One consequence of two decades of xenophobia governance by denial and displacement is, in fact, intensified xenophobia on the ground as there is no countervailing discourse about the benefits of migration. The police and justice system seem generally unable or unwilling to bring perpetrators of xenophobic violence to book and xenophobic sentiment is licensed by policies towards refugee protection and migrants in the informal sector that are generally extremely hostile to both (Crush et al., 2017). At best, the authorities (aided and abetted by some international organizations) have brokered various deals to limit the number of migrants working in the informal sector; a dispute resolution move that Gastrow (2018) finds unconstitutional. With official policies of xenophobia denialism and blaming in place, there seems little hope that South Africa will address one of the core commitments of the Global Compact on Migration; that is, "to, condemn and counter expressions, acts and manifestations of…xenophobia and related intolerance." Indeed, if xenophobia does not exist, then, by definition, there is nothing to condemn and counter. In this environment, the consequences for migrants themselves will continue to be extremely deleterious and deadly.

REFERENCES

1. Adibe, J. (2017). "Impact of Xenophobic Attacks against Africans in India on Afro-India Relations." *Journal of African Foreign Affairs*, 4: 85-97.

2. Ahuja, K., Banerjee, D., Chaudhary, K. and Gidwani, C. (2020). "Fear, Xenophobia and Collectivism as Predictors of Well-Being During Coronavirus Disease 2019: An Empirical Study from India." *International Journal of Social Psychiatry* (online).

3. Akinola, A. (ed.) (2018). *The Political Economy of Xenophobia in Africa* (Cham: Springer).

4. Arbour, L. (2018). "Migration and Development: A Virtuous Circle." *Great Insights*, 7: 4-7.

5. AU (African Union) (2006). "Country Review Report: Republic of South Africa." African Peer Review Mechanism, Midrand.

6. Auger, E., Blondin-Gravel, R., de la Sablonnière, R. and Taylor, D. (2011). "Construction of the Xenophobia Scale 2010." Report for Southern African Migration Project, Université de Montréal and McGill University, Montreal.

7. Bauer, N. (2013). "Diepsloot: Crime, Xenophobia – Or Both?" *Mail & Guardian*, 28 May.

8. Bekker, S. (2015). "Violent Xenophobic Episodes in South Africa, 2008 and 2015." *African Human Mobility Review*, 1: 229-252.

9. Bongmba, E. (2004). "Reflections on Thabo Mbeki's African Renaissance." *Journal of Southern African Studies*, 30(2): 291-316.

10. Burke, J. (2019). "'We Are A Target': Wave of Xenophobic Attacks Sweep Johannesburg." *The Guardian* 10 September.

11. Campbell, E. and Crush, J. (2015). "'They Don't Want Foreigners': Zimbabwean Migration and Xenophobia in Botswana." *Crossings: Journal of Migration and Culture*, 6: 159-80.

12. Castillo, R. and Amoah, P. (2020). "Africans in Post-COVID-19 Pandemic China: Is There a Future for China's 'New Minority'?" *Asian Ethnicity*, 21: 560-565.

13. Chan, C. and Strabucchi, M. (2020). "Many-Faced Orientalism: Racism and Xenophobia in a Time of the Novel Coronavirus in Chile." *Asian Ethnicity* (online)

14. Claassen, C. (2017). "Explaining South African Xenophobia." Afrobarometer Working Paper No. 173, Cape Town.

15. Constitutional Court (2016). "Lawyers for Human Rights v Minister in the Presidency and Others." At: http://www.saflii.org/za/cases/ZACC/2016/45.html

16. Crush, J. (2001). "The Dark Side of Democracy: Migration, Xenophobia and Human Rights in South Africa." *International Migration*, 38: 103-133.

17. Crush, J. (2008). *The Perfect Storm: The Realities of Xenophobia in Contemporary South Africa*. SAMP Migration Policy Series No. 50, Cape Town.

18. Crush, J. and Pendleton, W. (2007). "Mapping Hostilities: The Geography of Xenophobia in Southern Africa." *South African Geographical Journal*, 89: 64-82.

19. Crush, J. and Ramachandran, S. (2010). "Migration, Xenophobia and Human Development." *Journal of Human Development and Capabilities*, 11: 209-228.

20. Crush, J. and Ramachandran, S. (2014). *Xenophobic Violence in South Africa: Denialism, Minimalism, Realism*. SAMP Migration Policy Series No. 66, Cape Town.

21. Crush, J. and Ramachandran, S. (2015). "Doing Business with Xenophobia." In J. Crush, A. Chikanda and C. Skinner (eds.), *Mean Streets: Migration, Xenophobia and Informality in South Africa* (Ottawa: IDRC), pp. 25-59.

22. Crush, J., Chikanda, A. and Skinner, C. (eds.) (2015). *Mean Streets: Migration, Xenophobia and Informality in South Africa* (Ottawa: IDRC).

23. Crush, J., Ramachandran, S. and Pendleton, W. (2013). *Soft Targets: Xenophobia, Public Violence and Changing Attitudes to Migrants in South Africa After May 2008*. SAMP Migration Policy Series No. 64, Cape Town.

24. Crush, J., Skinner, C. and Stulgaitis, M. (2017). "Benign Neglect or Active Destruction? A Critical Analysis of Refugee and Informal Sector Policy and Practice in South Africa." *African Human Mobility Review*, 3(2): 751-782.

25. Dambrun, M., Taylor, D., McDonald, D., Crush, J. and Méot, A. (2006). "The Relative Deprivation-Gratification Continuum and the Attitudes of South Africans toward Immigrants: A Test of the V-Curve Hypothesis." *Journal of Personality and Social Psychology*, 91: 1032-1044.

26. d'Appollonia, A. (2017). "Xenophobia, Racism and the Securitization of Immigration." In P. Bourbeau (ed.), *Handbook on Migration and Security* (Cheltenham: Edward Elgar), pp. 252-272.

27. de la Sablonnière, R., Taylor, D and Coulombe, S. (2007). "Construction of a Xenophobia Scale" Report for Southern African Migration Project, Université de Montréal and McGill University, Montreal.

28. Davis, R. (2015). "Xenophobic violence: Government walks the walk, but will it talk the talk?" *Daily Maverick*, 12 April.

29. Debrosee, R., Cooper, M., Taylor, D., de la Sablonnière, R. and Crush, J. (2016). "Fundamental Rights in the Rainbow Nation: Intergroup Contact, Threat, and Support for Newcomers' Rights in Post-Apartheid South Africa." *Peace and Conflict: Journal of Peace Psychology*, 22: 367-379.

30. de la Sablonnière, R., Auger, E., Taylor, D., Crush, J. and McDonald, D. (2013). "Social Change in South Africa: An Historical Approach to Relative Deprivation." *British Journal of Social Psychology*, 52: 703-25.

31. Desai, A. (2015). "Migrants and Violence in South Africa: The April 2015 Xenophobic Attacks in Durban." *Oriental Anthropologists*, 15: 247-259.

32. DHA (2017). *White Paper on International Migration for South Africa* (Pretoria). At: http://www.dha.gov.za/WhitePaperonInternationalMigration-20170602.pdf

33. Dodson, B. (2016). "Migration to South Africa Since 1994: Realities, Policies and Public Attitudes" In T. Kepe, M. Levin and B. von Lieres (eds.), *Domains of Freedom: Justice, Citizenship and Social Change in South Africa* (Cape Town: UCT Press), pp. 277-298.

34. Dube, G. (2013). "Afrophobia in Mzansi? Evidence from the 2013 South African Social Attitudes Survey." *Journal of Southern African Studies*, 44: 1005-1021.

35. Dube, G. (2019). "Black South Africans' Attitudes toward African Immigrants between 2008 and 2016." *Nationalism and Ethnic Politics*, 25: 191-210.

36. Facchini, G., Mayda, A. and Mendola, M. (2013). "What Drives Individual Attitudes towards Immigration in South Africa?" *Review of International Economics*, 21: 326-341.

37. Fassin, D. and Schneider, H. (2003). "The Politics of AIDS in South Africa: Beyond the Controversies." *British Medical Journal*, 326(7387): 495-497.

38. Fiddian-Qasmiyeh, E. (2020). "Recentering the South in Studies of Migration." *Migration and Society*, 3: 1-18.

39. Finnan, D. (2015). "Immigration camps not the solution to stopping South Africa's xenophobic attacks." *Radio France Internationale/AllAfrica*, 16 April.

40. Fourchard, L. and Segatti, A. (2015). "The Everyday Politics of Exclusion and Inclusion in Africa." *Africa*, 85: 2-12.

41. Gastrow, V. (2018). *Problematizing the Foreign Shop: Justifications for Restricting the Migrant Spaza Sector in South Africa*. SAMP Migration Policy Series No. 80, Cape Town.

42. Gerber, J. (2019). "Xenophobia? What xenophobia? Ministers prefer the term 'criminality'." *News24*, 11 September.

43. Gill, B. and Danns, G. (2018). "Xenophobia in Africa, Latin America, and the Caribbean: Definitions, Theories, and Experiences." In S. Abidde and B. Gill (eds.), *Africans and the Exiled Life: Migration, Culture, and Globalization* (New York: Rowman & Littlefield), pp. 143-160.

44. Gomes, C. (2014). "Xenophobia Online: Unmasking Singaporean Attitudes Towards 'Foreign Talent' Migrants." *Asian Ethnicity*, 15: 21-40.

45. Gordon, S. (2016a). "Xenophobia Across the Class Divide: South African Attitudes Towards Foreigners, 2003-2012." *Journal of Contemporary African Studies*, 33: 494-509.

46. Gordon, S. (2016b). "Welcoming Refugees in the Rainbow Nation: Contemporary Attitudes Towards Refugees in South Africa." *African Geographical Review*, 35: 1-17.

47. Gordon, S. (2017a). "Waiting for the Barbarians: A Public Opinion Analysis of South African Attitudes towards International Migrants." *Ethnic and Racial Studies*, 40: 1700–1719.

48. Gordon, S. (2017b). "A Desire for Isolation? Mass Public Attitudes in South Africa." *Journal of Immigrant & Refugee Studies*, 15: 18-35.

49. Gordon, S. (2018). "Who Is Welcoming and Who Is Not? An Attitudinal Analysis of Anti-Immigrant Sentiment in South Africa." *South African Review of Sociology*, 49: 72-90.

50. Gordon, S. (2019). "A Violent Minority? A Quantitative Analysis of Those Engaged in Anti-Immigrant Violence in South Africa" *South African Geographical Journal*, 101: 269-283.

51. Gordon, S. and Maharaj, B. (2015). "Neighbourhood-Level Social Capital and Anti-Immigrant Prejudice in an African Context: An Individual-Level Analysis of Attitudes Towards Immigrants in South Africa." *Commonwealth and Comparative Politics*, 53: 197-219.

52. Gordon, S. (2020a). "Understanding Xenophobic Hate Crime in South Africa." *Journal of Public Affairs*, 20(3): e2076.

53. Gordon, S. (2020b). "Understanding the Attitude-Behaviour Relationship: A Quantitative Analysis of Public Participation in Anti-Immigrant Violence in South Africa." *South African Journal of Psychology*, 50: 103-114.

54. Gorinas, C. and Pytliková, M. (2018). "The Influence of Attitudes toward Immigrants on International Migration." *International Migration Review*, 51(2): 416-451.

55. Hassim, S., Kupe, T. and Worby, E. (eds.) (2008). *Go Home or Die Here: Violence, Xenophobia and the Reinvention of Difference in South Africa* (Johannesburg: Wits University Press).

56. Hayem, J. (2013). "From May 2008 to 2011: Xenophobic Violence and National Subjectivity in South Africa" *Journal of Southern African Studies*, 39: 77–97.

57. Hiropoulos, A. (2019). "South Africa, Migration and Xenophobia: Deconstructing the Perceived Migration Crisis and Its Influence on the Xenophobic Reception of Migrants." *Contemporary Justice Review*, 23: 104-121.

58. HRW (2019). *'They Have Robbed Me of My Life': Xenophobic Violence Against Non-Nationals in South Africa* (Johannesburg: Human Rights Watch).

59. Isaacson, M. (2011). "Attacks on Foreigners are Xenophobic." *Sunday Independent*, 21 June.

60. Johnson, A. (2020). "Herman Mashaba Wants You to Forget." *Africa is a Country*, 8 July.

61. Jones, T. (2020). "Xenophobia in Spite of Citizenship: Seasonal Migrant Workers in Brazil," *A Contracorriente: una revista de estudios latinoamericanos*, 17: 54-68.

62. Jordaan, N. (2015). "Operation Fiela 'demoralizes and dehumanizes' migrants." *Sunday Times*, 22 July.

63. Landau, L. (ed.) (2012). *Exorcising the Demons Within: Xenophobia, Violence and Statecraft in Contemporary South Africa* (Johannesburg: Wits University Press).

64. LHR (Lawyers for Human Rights) (2015). "Press Statement: Civil Society Organizations Address Media on the Ongoing Raids Targeting Foreign Nationals." Lawyers for Human Rights, Pretoria.

65. Matsinhe, D. (2011). *Apartheid Vertigo: The Rise in Discrimination against Africans in South Africa* (Farnham: Ashgate).

66. Mbeki, T. (2008). "Address of the President of South Africa at the National Tribute in Remembrance of the Victims of Attacks on Foreign Nationals." At: http://www.info.gov.za/speeches/2008/08070410451001.htm

67. Merten, M. (2015). "Steps to Halt Xenophobic Violence." *Daily News*, 15 April.

68. Meseguer, C. and Kemmerling, A. (2018). "What Do You Fear? Anti-Immigrant Sentiment in Latin America." *International Migration Review*, 52: 236-272.

69. Miran-Guyon, M. (2016). "Islam In and Out: Cosmopolitan Patriotism and Xenophobia Among Muslims in Côte D'Ivoire." *Africa*, 86: 447-471.

70. Misago, J-P. (2016). "Migration, Governance and Violent Exclusion: Exploring the Determinants of Xenophobic Violence in Post-Apartheid South Africa." PhD Thesis, University of the Witwatersrand, Johannesburg.

71. Misago, J-P. (2017). "Politics by Other Means? The Political Economy of Xenophobic Violence in Post-Apartheid South Africa." *The Black Scholar*, 47: 40-53.

72. Mlilo, S. and Misago, J-P. (2019). *Xenophobic Violence in South Africa: 1994-2018. An Overview*. African Centre for Migration & Society (ACMS), Johannesburg.

73. Mothibi, K., Roelofse, C. and Tshivhase, T. (2015). "Xenophobic Attacks on Foreign Shop Owners and Street Vendors in Louis Trichardt Central Business District, Limpopo Province." *Journal for Transdisciplinary Research in Southern Africa*, 11: 151-162.

74. Musuva, C. (2015). "International Migration, Xenophobia and the South African State" PhD Thesis, Stellenbosch University, Stellenbosch.

75. Nattrass, N. (2003). *The Moral Economy of AIDS in South Africa* (Cambridge: Cambridge University Press).

76. Neocosmos, M. (2008). "The Politics of Fear and the Fear of Politics: Reflections on Xenophobic Violence in South Africa." *Journal of Asian and African Studies*, 43: 586-594.

77. Ngcamu, B. and Mantzaris, E. (2019). "Xenophobic Violence and Criminality in the KwaZulu-Natal Townships." *Journal for Transdisciplinary Research in Southern Africa*, 15: 1-8.

78. Ngubane, S. (2015). "Anti-Xenophobia March: Chaos in Durban." *IOL*, 9 April.

79. News24 (2015). "Attacks on Foreigners Not Xenophobia: Committee." *News24*, 10 July.

80. Nicolson, G. (2015). "Parliamentary Report on Xenophobic Violence Talks a Lot, Says Very Little." *Daily Maverick*, 24 November.

81. NPC (National Planning Commission) (2012). *Our Future – Make It Work: National Development Plan 2030* (Pretoria).

82. Nyamnjoh, F. (2006). *Insiders and Outsiders: Citizenship and Xenophobia in Contemporary Southern Africa* (London: Zed Books).

83. Patel, K. (2013). "SA government reiterates: It's crime, not xenophobia." *Daily Maverick*, 8 June.

84. Pécoud, A. (2020). "Narrating an Ideal Migration World? An Analysis of the Global Compact for Safe, Orderly and Regular Migration." *Third World Quarterly* (online).

85. Peterie, M. and Neil, D. (2020). "Xenophobia Towards Asylum Seekers: A Survey of Social Theories." *Journal of Sociology*, 56: 23-35.

86. PJC (Parliamentary Joint Committee) (2015). *Report of the Ad Hoc Joint Committee on Probing Violence Against Foreign Nationals*. Cape Town: South African Parliament.

87. PMG (Parliamentary Monitoring Group) (2015). "Inter-Ministerial Committee Briefing." At https://pmg.org.za/committee-meeting/21805/

88. Potgieter, E. (2019). *SA Reconciliation Barometer 2019* (Cape Town: Institute for Justice and Reconciliation).

89. Ramachandran, S. (2019). "Border Disorder: 'Irregular Bangladeshis', Xenophobia and Crimmigration Control in India." PhD Thesis, Wilfrid Laurier University, Waterloo.

90. Ramachandran, S., Crush, J. and Tawodzera, G. (2017). "Security Risk and Xenophobia in the Urban Informal Sector." *African Human Mobility Review*, 3(2): 855-878.

91. Reny, T. and Barreto, M. (2020). "Xenophobia in the Time of Pandemic: Othering, Anti-Asian Attitudes, and COVID-19." *Politics, Groups and Identities* (online).

92. Rensmann, L. and Miller, J. (2017). "Xenophobia and Anti-Immigrant Politics" In R. Denemark and R. Marlin-Bennett (eds.), *The International Studies Encyclopedia* (Oxford: Wiley-Blackwell).

93. RSA (Republic of South Africa) (2013). "Statement on the Cabinet Meeting of 29 May 2013." At http://www.gcis.gov.za/content/newsroom/media-releases/cabinet-state-ments/statement-cabinet-meeting-29May2013

94. RSA (Republic of South Africa) (2019). *National Action Plan (NAP) to Combat Racism, Racial Discrimination, Xenophobia and Related Intolerance* (Pretoria).

95. Ruedin, D. (2019). "Attitudes to Immigrants in South Africa: Personality and Vulner-ability." *Journal of Ethnic and Migration Studies*, 45: 1108-1126.

96. Sapa (2010). "Minister Tackles Xenophobic Attacks." *IOL News*, 12 July.

97. SRG (Special Reference Group) (2015). *Report on Migration and Community Integration in KwaZulu-Natal* (Pietermaritzburg: Provincial Government of KwaZulu-Natal).

98. Steinberg, J. (2012). "Security and Disappointment: Policing, Freedom and Xenophobia in South Africa." *British Journal of Criminology*, 52: 345-360.

99. Steinberg, J. (2018). "Xenophobia and Collective Violence in South Africa: A Note of Skepticism About the Scapegoat." *African Studies Review*, 61: 119-134.

100. Tevera, D. (2013). "African Migrants, Xenophobia and Urban Violence in Post-Apartheid South Africa." *Alternation*, 7: 9-26.

101. Ullah, A., Lee, S., Hassan, N. and Nawaz, F. (2020). "Xenophobia in the GCC Countries: Migrants' Desire and Distress." *Global Affairs*, 6: 203-223.

102. UN (2020). *Global Compact for Safe, Orderly and Regular Migration*. UN General Assembly Resolution, New York.

103. Whitaker, B. (2015). "Playing the Immigration Card: The Politics of Exclusion in Côte d'Ivoire and Ghana." *Commonwealth & Comparative Politics*, 53(3): 274-293.

104. Yang, P. (2018). "Desiring 'Foreign Talent': Lack and Lacan in Anti-Immigrant Sentiments in Singapore." *Journal of Ethnic and Migration Studies*, 44: 1015-1031.

105. Zuma, J. (2015). "South Africa is not a Xenophobic Nation." *The Guardian*, 28 April.

MIGRATION POLICY SERIES

1 *Covert Operations: Clandestine Migration, Temporary Work and Immigration Policy in South Africa* (1997) ISBN 1-874864-51-9

2 *Riding the Tiger: Lesotho Miners and Permanent Residence in South Africa* (1997) ISBN 1-874864-52-7

3 *International Migration, Immigrant Entrepreneurs and South Africa's Small Enterprise Economy* (1997) ISBN 1-874864-62-4

4 *Silenced by Nation Building: African Immigrants and Language Policy in the New South Africa* (1998) ISBN 1-874864-64-0

5 *Left Out in the Cold? Housing and Immigration in the New South Africa* (1998) ISBN 1-874864-68-3

6 *Trading Places: Cross-Border Traders and the South African Informal Sector* (1998) ISBN 1-874864-71-3

7 *Challenging Xenophobia: Myth and Realities about Cross-Border Migration in Southern Africa* (1998) ISBN 1-874864-70-5

8 *Sons of Mozambique: Mozambican Miners and Post-Apartheid South Africa* (1998) ISBN 1-874864-78-0

9 *Women on the Move: Gender and Cross-Border Migration to South Africa* (1998) ISBN 1-874864-82-9

10 *Namibians on South Africa: Attitudes Towards Cross-Border Migration and Immigration Policy* (1998) ISBN 1-874864-84-5

11 *Building Skills: Cross-Border Migrants and the South African Construction Industry* (1999) ISBN 1-874864-84-5

12 *Immigration & Education: International Students at South African Universities and Technikons* (1999) ISBN 1-874864-89-6

13 *The Lives and Times of African Immigrants in Post-Apartheid South Africa* (1999) ISBN 1-874864-91-8

14 *Still Waiting for the Barbarians: South African Attitudes to Immigrants and Immigration* (1999) ISBN 1-874864-91-8

15 *Undermining Labour: Migrancy and Sub-Contracting in the South African Gold Mining Industry* (1999) ISBN 1-874864-91-8

16 *Borderline Farming: Foreign Migrants in South African Commercial Agriculture* (2000) ISBN 1-874864-97-7

17 *Writing Xenophobia: Immigration and the Press in Post-Apartheid South Africa* (2000) ISBN 1-919798-01-3

18 *Losing Our Minds: Skills Migration and the South African Brain Drain* (2000) ISBN 1-919798-03-x

19 *Botswana: Migration Perspectives and Prospects* (2000) ISBN 1-919798-04-8

20 *The Brain Gain: Skilled Migrants and Immigration Policy in Post-Apartheid South Africa* (2000) ISBN 1-919798-14-5

21 *Cross-Border Raiding and Community Conflict in the Lesotho-South African Border Zone* (2001) ISBN 1-919798-16-1

22 *Immigration, Xenophobia and Human Rights in South Africa* (2001) ISBN 1-919798-30-7

23 *Gender and the Brain Drain from South Africa* (2001) ISBN 1-919798-35-8

24 *Spaces of Vulnerability: Migration and HIV/AIDS in South Africa* (2002) ISBN 1-919798-38-2

25 *Zimbabweans Who Move: Perspectives on International Migration in Zimbabwe* (2002) ISBN 1-919798-40-4

26 *The Border Within: The Future of the Lesotho-South African International Boundary* (2002) ISBN 1-919798-41-2

27 *Mobile Namibia: Migration Trends and Attitudes* (2002) ISBN 1-919798-44-7

28 *Changing Attitudes to Immigration and Refugee Policy in Botswana* (2003) ISBN 1-919798-47-1

29 *The New Brain Drain from Zimbabwe* (2003) ISBN 1-919798-48-X

30 *Regionalizing Xenophobia? Citizen Attitudes to Immigration and Refugee Policy in Southern Africa* (2004) ISBN 1-919798-53-6

31 *Migration, Sexuality and HIV/AIDS in Rural South Africa* (2004) ISBN 1-919798-63-3

32 *Swaziland Moves: Perceptions and Patterns of Modern Migration* (2004) ISBN 1-919798-67-6

33 *HIV/AIDS and Children's Migration in Southern Africa* (2004) ISBN 1-919798-70-6

34 *Medical Leave: The Exodus of Health Professionals from Zimbabwe* (2005) ISBN 1-919798-74-9

35 *Degrees of Uncertainty: Students and the Brain Drain in Southern Africa* (2005) ISBN 1-919798-84-6

36 *Restless Minds: South African Students and the Brain Drain* (2005) ISBN 1-919798-82-X

37 *Understanding Press Coverage of Cross-Border Migration in Southern Africa since 2000* (2005) ISBN 1-919798-91-9

38 *Northern Gateway: Cross-Border Migration Between Namibia and Angola* (2005) ISBN 1-919798-92-7

39 *Early Departures: The Emigration Potential of Zimbabwean Students* (2005) ISBN 1-919798-99-4

40 *Migration and Domestic Workers: Worlds of Work, Health and Mobility in Johannesburg* (2005) ISBN 1-920118-02-0

41 *The Quality of Migration Services Delivery in South Africa* (2005) ISBN 1-920118-03-9

42 *States of Vulnerability: The Future Brain Drain of Talent to South Africa* (2006) ISBN 1-920118-07-1

43 *Migration and Development in Mozambique: Poverty, Inequality and Survival* (2006) ISBN 1-920118-10-1

44 *Migration, Remittances and Development in Southern Africa* (2006) ISBN 1-920118-15-2

45 *Medical Recruiting: The Case of South African Health Care Professionals* (2007) ISBN 1-920118-47-0

46 *Voices From the Margins: Migrant Women's Experiences in Southern Africa* (2007) ISBN 1-920118-50-0

47 *The Haemorrhage of Health Professionals From South Africa: Medical Opinions* (2007) ISBN 978-1-920118-63-1

48 *The Quality of Immigration and Citizenship Services in Namibia* (2008) ISBN 978-1-920118-67-9

49 *Gender, Migration and Remittances in Southern Africa* (2008) ISBN 978-1-920118-70-9

50 *The Perfect Storm: The Realities of Xenophobia in Contemporary South Africa* (2008) ISBN 978-1-920118-71-6

51 *Migrant Remittances and Household Survival in Zimbabwe* (2009) ISBN 978-1-920118-92-1

52 *Migration, Remittances and 'Development' in Lesotho* (2010) ISBN 978-1-920409-26-5

53 *Migration-Induced HIV and AIDS in Rural Mozambique and Swaziland* (2011) ISBN 978-1-920409-49-4

54 *Medical Xenophobia: Zimbabwean Access to Health Services in South Africa* (2011) ISBN 978-1-920409-63-0

55 *The Engagement of the Zimbabwean Medical Diaspora* (2011) ISBN 978-1-920409-64-7

56 *Right to the Classroom: Educational Barriers for Zimbabweans in South Africa* (2011) ISBN 978-1-920409-68-5

57 *Patients Without Borders: Medical Tourism and Medical Migration in Southern Africa* (2012) ISBN 978-1-920409-74-6

58 *The Disengagement of the South African Medical Diaspora* (2012) ISBN 978-1-920596-00-2

59 *The Third Wave: Mixed Migration from Zimbabwe to South Africa* (2012) ISBN 978-1-920596-01-9

60 *Linking Migration, Food Security and Development* (2012) ISBN 978-1-920596-02-6

61 *Unfriendly Neighbours: Contemporary Migration from Zimbabwe to Botswana* (2012) ISBN 978-1-920596-16-3

62 *Heading North: The Zimbabwean Diaspora in Canada* (2012) ISBN 978-1-920596-03-3

63 *Dystopia and Disengagement: Diaspora Attitudes Towards South Africa* (2012) ISBN 978-1-920596-04-0

64 *Soft Targets: Xenophobia, Public Violence and Changing Attitudes to Migrants in South Africa after May 2008* (2013) ISBN 978-1-920596-05-7

65 *Brain Drain and Regain: Migration Behaviour of South African Medical Professionals* (2014) ISBN 978-1-920596-07-1

66 *Xenophobic Violence in South Africa: Denialism, Minimalism, Realism* (2014) ISBN 978-1-920596-08-8

67 *Migrant Entrepreneurship Collective Violence and Xenophobia in South Africa* (2014) ISBN 978-1-920596-09-5

68 *Informal Migrant Entrepreneurship and Inclusive Growth in South Africa, Zimbabwe and Mozambique* (2015) ISBN 978-1-920596-10-1

69 *Calibrating Informal Cross-Border Trade in Southern Africa* (2015) ISBN 978-1-920596-13-2

70 *International Migrants and Refugees in Cape Town's Informal Economy* (2016) ISBN 978-1-920596-15-6

71 *International Migrants in Johannesburg's Informal Economy* (2016) ISBN 978-1-920596-18-7

72 *Food Remittances: Migration and Food Security in Africa* (2016) ISBN 978-1-920596-19-4

73 *Informal Entrepreneurship and Cross-Border Trade in Maputo, Mozambique* (2016) ISBN 978-1-920596-20-0

74 *Informal Entrepreneurship and Cross-Border Trade between Zimbabwe and South Africa* (2017) ISBN 978-1-920596-29-3

75 *Competition or Co-operation? South African and Migrant Entrepreneurs in Johannesburg* (2017) ISBN 978-1-920596-30-9

76 *Refugee Entrepreneurial Economies in Urban South Africa* (2017) ISBN 978-1-920596-35-4

77 *Living With Xenophobia: Zimbabwean Informal Enterprise in South Africa* (2017) ISBN 978-1-920596-37-8

78 *Comparing Refugees and South Africans in the Urban Informal Sector* (2017) ISBN 978-1-920596-38-5

79 *Rendering South Africa Undesirable: A Critique of Refugee and Informal Sector Policy* (2017) ISBN 978-1-920596-40-8

80 *Problematizing the Foreign Shop: Justifications for Restricting the Migrant Spaza Sector in South Africa* (2018) ISBN 978-1-920596-43-9

81 *Rethinking the South African Medical Brain Drain Narrative* (2020) ISBN 978-1-920596-45-3

www.ingramcontent.com/pod-product-compliance
Lightning Source LLC
Chambersburg PA
CBHW080556270326
41929CB00019B/3332